I am a Humpback Whale

Aaron Carr

MEDIA ENHANCED BOOKS
AV²
BY WEIGL™
ADDED VALUE • AUDIO VISUAL

Go to **www.av2books.com**, and enter this book's unique code.

BOOK CODE

Z 1 3 2 4 1

AV² by Weigl brings you media enhanced books that support active learning.

AV² provides enriched content that supplements and complements this book. Weigl's AV² books strive to create inspired learning and engage young minds in a total learning experience.

Your AV² Media Enhanced books come alive with...

Audio
Listen to sections of the book read aloud.

Video
Watch informative video clips.

Embedded Weblinks
Gain additional information for research.

Try This!
Complete activities and hands-on experiments.

Key Words
Study vocabulary, and complete a matching word activity.

Quizzes
Test your knowledge.

Slide Show
View images and captions, and prepare a presentation.

... and much, much more!

Published by AV² by Weigl
350 5th Avenue, 59th Floor New York, NY 10118
Website: www.av2books.com   www.weigl.com

Library of Congress Cataloging-in-Publication Data
Carr, Aaron.
 Humpback whale / Aaron Carr.
    pages cm. -- (I am)
 Audience: Grades K to 3.
 ISBN 978-1-62127-284-7 (hardcover : alk. paper) -- ISBN 978-1-62127-290-8 (softcover : alk. paper)
 1. Humpback whale--Juvenile literature. I. Title.
 QL737.C424C36 2014
 599.5'25--dc23
                    2012046233

Printed in the United States of America in North Mankato, Minnesota
1 2 3 4 5 6 7 8 9 0 17 16 15 14 13

032013
WEP300113

Senior Editor: Aaron Carr   Art Director: Terry Paulhus

Weigl acknowledges Getty Images as the primary image supplier for this title.

I am a Humpback Whale

In this book, I will teach you about

- myself
- my food
- my home
- my family

and much more!

I am a humpback whale.

I live underwater,
but I breathe air.

I am as big
as a school bus.

I can eat up to 3,000 pounds of food in one day.

I live in a group called a pod. There are three whales in my pod.

13

I sing a song
to talk to other whales.

I was 13 feet long
when I was born.

I swim more than 10,000 miles every year.

I can be seen
on whale watching tours.

I am a humpback whale.

HUMPBACK WHALE FACTS

These pages provide detailed information that expands on the interesting facts found in the book. They are intended to be used by adults as a learning support to help young readers round out their knowledge of each amazing animal featured in the *I Am* series.

Pages 4–5

I am a humpback whale.

I am a humpback whale. The scientific name for the humpback whale means "big-winged New Englander." It got this name because it was first classified near New England, and for its large pectoral fins. The humpback whale has two pectoral fins. Each can be up to 15 feet (4.6 meters) long.

Pages 6–7

I live underwater, but I breathe air.

I live underwater, but I breathe air. Humpback whales live in all oceans of the world, but prefer to stay near coastlines, and will even venture into bays and rivers. Humpbacks breathe air through two blowholes on the top of the head. They can hold their breath for up to 30 minutes.

Pages 8–9

I am as big as a school bus.

I am as big as a school bus. Humpback whales are among the largest animals on Earth. They can grow to 50 feet (16 m) long and can weigh up to 40 tons (36 tonnes). The fluke, or tail fin, can be up to 15 feet (4.5 m) wide. Female humpbacks, or cows, are larger than male humpback whales, called bulls.

Pages 10–11

I can eat up to 3,000 pounds of food in one day.

I can eat up to 3,000 pounds (1,360 kilograms) of food in one day. Humpbacks are a type of baleen whale. Instead of teeth, such whales have long, hair-like strands of keratin. This is the material that makes up fingernails. These hair-like strands, called baleen, filter food from the water. Humpbacks eat krill, plankton, and small fish.

Pages 12–13

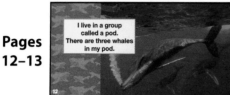

I live in a group called a pod. Humpback whale pods generally range in size from two to three. Pods of fifteen whales have been documented. Pods are not permanent groups, and humpbacks will regularly leave a pod, joining a new one later. Males may act as escorts for a cow with a calf.

Pages 14–15

I sing a song to talk to other whales. The humpback whale makes a wide range of sounds, which it strings together into long, complex songs. These songs can last up to 35 minutes. Only males sing. It is believed the songs are used to attract mates. Underwater, these songs can be heard more than 20 miles (30 kilometers) away.

Pages 16–17

I was 13 feet (4 m) long when I was born. A mother will carry her baby for up to one year before giving birth. Humpbacks give birth during the winter, every two to three years. Calves grow continuously for up to 10 years before they reach their adult size. Newborns can drink up to 100 pounds (45 kg) of milk in one day.

Pages 18–19

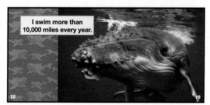

I swim more than 10,000 miles (16,000 km) every year. Humpback whales are migratory animals. Each winter, many whales will migrate up to 5000 miles (8,000 km) one way, to their breeding grounds in warmer waters. That is more than 10,000 miles (16,000 km) round trip.

Pages 20–21

I can be seen on whale watching tours. The humpback whale is the most acrobatic of all whale species. They often breach, or jump out of the water, and will slap the water with their great flukes. For this reason, humpback whales are commonly pursued by whale watching boats.

KEY WORDS

Research has shown that as much as 65 percent of all written material published in English is made up of 300 words. These 300 words cannot be taught using pictures or learned by sounding them out. They must be recognized by sight. This book contains 37 common sight words to help young readers improve their reading fluency and comprehension. This book also teaches young readers several important content words, such as proper nouns. These words are paired with pictures to aid in learning and improve understanding.

Page	Sight Words First Appearance
4	a, am, I
6	air, but, live
8	as, big, school
10	can, day, eat, food, in, of, one, to, up
12	are, group, my, there, three
14	other, song, talk
16	feet, long, was, when
18	every, miles, more, than, year
20	be, on

Page	Content Words First Appearance
4	humpback whale
8	bus
10	pounds
12	pod
20	tours